Dowsing For Prisoners

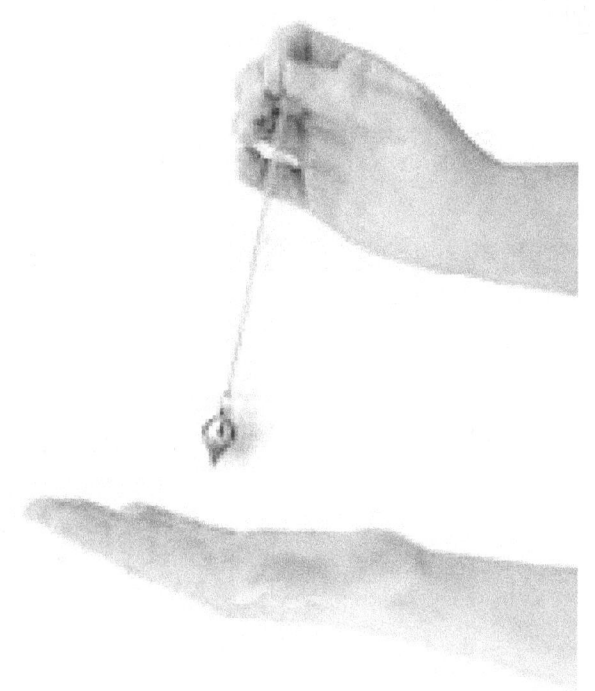

Answers From Above

Rev. Mike Wanner

Copyright

August 25, 2017

Reverend Mike Wanner

Selected Images Used by License

Table Of Contents

Table Of Contents 3
Introduction 4
1 - Dowsing For Prisoners 5
2 - Welcome to Dowsing for Prisoners 7
3 - Purpose Of This Book 8
4 - Dowsing And Test Prep 10
5 - Dowsing And Research 11
6 - Please Know 14
7 - THE TREASURE 18
8 - LEGAL NOTICE 21
9 - Thank You 22
10 - Don't Worry Ever 23
11 - Resource Books 24
12 - Angels Please Prayers 26
13 - Private Channeling 27
14 - Reverend Mike Wanner 28

Introduction

Some sources report that in America alone there are more than 2.3 million people in jail.

All the intellect in all those residents may not be used well because the owners of the brains are incarcerated.

I, like most people, was oblivious to that fact until I was invited to look into it. I started channeling Angel Raphael in 2013 and began releasing little message sets as they came through.

In message set 16 of the Angel Raphael Speaks Series there was a message that has remained floating in my head since as topic for my writing.

The message I resisted was an invitation to visit jail energetically. Here is that message –

"I asked Mike to Step into Prison Energetically

I have asked Mike to get the address and location within a prison of a designated space so he can visit energetically and receive feedback for us to consider. Whether he will have time, interest or opportunity to do this will be interesting to see. As he writes this, he is not thrilled with the idea. We are already consuming a lot of his time." ARS16

1 - Dowsing For Prisoners
&
Students Of Possibility

The Future may look kind of bleak because the slump that prison has created may have taken you to new lows in your thinking about your future.

BUT

You are still a child of the God Most High.

Have You Been A Good Child Of God?

Could You Have Been Better?

Would You Do Better If You Got Another Chance?

Would You Like One?

Every Day Is One!

Nothing
Is
Everything

But

Everything
Is
Nothing

Ask On High
Readout Via A
Washer and A String?
Maybe.

2 - Welcome to Dowsing for Prisoners

Dowsing is real, and its' effectiveness is subject to the skill of the dowser. You can potentially increase your information gathering process exponentially and gain an edge over any conventional methods you use to gather, sort and absorb information.

While I will move right into the educational possibilities that might be helpful today for those taking classes, I will withhold the real treasure until the end of the document.

It is an excellent idea to learn how to dowse subtly since there will be many times that you can use decision assistance where you would not like to be obvious.

BASIC RULE

There is one rule that a new dowser needs to know!

Dowse for Need, not Greed

You cannot predict the future.

3 - Purpose Of This Book

The Purpose of this Booklet is multifaceted:

1. To simplify test prep for those that study dowsing.
2. To simplify research for those that study dowsing.
3. To help support Dowsing and this valuable information for future generations by allowing the young and young at heart to learn this powerful technique.
4. To share the awesome power of the Age of Cause.

ORGANIZATIONS

The American Society of Dowsers (www.dowsers.org), The Canadian Society of Dowsers (www.canadiandowsers.org), The Canadian Society of Questers (www.questers.ca) and The Toronto Dowsers (www.dowsers.info) are all great organizations that have educational programs.

Recommended Reading –

LETTER TO ROBIN

The American Society of Dowsers has a wonderful bookstore with every tool you could conceive. One such product is a little booklet called "Letter To Robin" which is a small but dense information Text and/or workbook which was written to be user-friendly. The book can also be downloaded on line from www.LettertoRobin.org.

PRACTICE, PRACTICE, PRACTICE

Dowsing can be learned quickly, but practice is the key to accuracy.

Generally speaking, when one has an interest in an outcome, it is best to have someone else dowse for you. That being said, One must decide the merits of proceeding without that luxury.

4 - Dowsing And Test Prep

When it is crunch time, and you need to get ready, you want to study the most relevant information that will be on the test. Use the Binary Acceleration below to ask what might be picked by the instructor. Skill should b,e exercised to label segments of your material so that the dowsing is most effective.

Dowsing And Tests

Dowsing Techniques can vary. It can be done in many ways. If the reader desires to make occasional Dowsing efforts during academic tests, one must be aware of and take responsibility for what is considered cheating by the testing authority. Some may look at you as accessing information that you know and others may not. There are also device-less dowsing techniques which are not in Letter to Robin that you may wish to study after you have some experience.

5 - Dowsing And Research

A Very consistent application for dowsing is in the research arena. Dowsing can help you select the optimal books for your papers and help you to find the best resources quickly.

THE BINARY ACCELERATION EFFECT

BOOK SELECTION

Computers are comparable to dowsing in that they both work on "Yes" and "No." In the early programming days the selection went **IF** this **THEN** that **ELSE** _____. So computers and Dowsing are both Binary

If you are a good dowser, you can get a lot of answers in a little time as long as you have a good question that you want to be taken literally.

Picking from a library card deck or a computer screen can be simplified when you point at a Reference and asks if that text has the optimal Information for the assignment.

After looking at many references, one can go the bookcase and select the books knowing that success is most likely.

Further reduction can be made by multiple group disqualifications. Perhaps you would ask a series of questions about each book like:

1. Is the information that I seek in the first half of this book?

2. If yes, Is the information that I want to be located within the first half of the half represented by the answer to question 1?

3. If Question 1 answer is No, Is the information that I seek in the second half of the half represented by the answer to question 1?

4. Is the information that I seek in the second half of the book referenced in question 1?

5. If yes, Is the information that I want to be located within the first half of the second half of the book represented by the answer to question 1?

6. If no, Is the information that I want to be located with the second half of the second half of the book represented by the answer to question 1?

7. Continuing to reduce until you get down to the page that has the information that you need

6 - Please Know

There is no magic here and no guarantees. You get what you get and you are in charge of your life and your dowsing efforts.

ANSWERS ARE NOT ABSOLUTE

Within you there is enormous potential, ignoring it serves you not but moving towards it does. Even a "wrong" answer can move you in a direction that leads to an intersection that can access your destination. On airplanes, you are reminded that the nearest exit may be behind you. Thankfully, dowsing is a skill that dowsers continue to polish.

Be open to it all but don't wait for an engraved invitation. **You are in Charge. Keep questioning** to verify the answers.

ANSWERS ARE NOT PERMANENT

Follow any dowsing answer only as long as it stimulates your creative thought and then follows that thought pathway to Your highest good. Stay aware that after you make any decision, the wisdom of each decision is influenced by subsequent information factors that are decided by others and which you could never predict.

ABOUT YOUR QUESTIONS

1. They should be precise and not subject to misinterpretation.
2. Write them out on a piece of paper.
3. It is best not to be vague like:
    Am I doing the right thing?
    Will I be successful?
    Did I do the right thing?
4. The best premises/questions would be something specific like:

Will I earn a $100 or more during a particular time?

Am I on the correct path to my highest good?

Something measurable?

It is a good idea to throw in some test items that you know the answer to. It is best to be very specific. The best test questions would be something that is verifiable somewhere.

5. Do not try to ask fortune telling type Questions. Ask only in the present tense.

PROGRAMMING YOUR DOWSING SYSTEM

It is wise to program your dowsing so that reliability is optimized. The reference text has multiple programs, and I recommend that you install

At least the "Primary Program" and the "May I, Can I, should I" Program.

TRUSTING YOUR DOWSING

Like anything else in your life, trust has to be developed. Development takes hard work.

7 - THE TREASURE

AGE OF CAUSE

Long before I was dowsing, I was already on my spiritual path and consulted with a Shaman for a "Soul Retrieval." The concept involves a revisiting of life experiences and the reclaiming of the pieces of the Soul that may have been lost during dramatic life events. The shaman spent an hour and a half going through a whole ritual to the point where she could tell me about the pivotal experience in my life that caused the creation of a pattern which had plagued me for years. She found out that when I was eleven, and my father died, a pattern started. The pattern was a type of paralysis that came up when I was under stress. It caused me to go into a loop with the mantra "I don't know where I am, I don't know where I am going."

That information from the shaman gave me a new freedom because I could then deal with the issue. I could take charge of my life once again by acknowledging the pattern and declaring that it had no power over me. WOW

The Age of Cause is a powerful question to ask. I have found that a lot of people have issues/illnesses/problems that they don't know where they came from.

HOW TO DO THIS

It is similar to the Binary Acceleration that I discussed earlier.

Learning about the "Age Of Cause" has allowed me to help others as the Shaman had helped me. Finding the age is very simple with Dowsing. Here is what you do:

1. Ask the typical "Can I, May I, Should I? " dowsing questions and if you get a yes, proceed.
2. Guess/determine the age that is about half the client's age.

3. Dowse if the Age of Cause (AOC) is less than or more than that age?
4. Depending on the answer, Dowse if the AOC is less than or more than ½ the #3 answer.
5. Depending on the response, Dowse if the AOC is less than or more than ½ the #4 Answer.
6. Depending on the response, Dowse if the AOC is less than or more than ½ the #5 Answer.
7. Continue until you get to a single age, Ask if that is the AOC.

Once you have the Age of Cause, you can work around that with Bodywork and energy work to help the person find their way back to wholeness.

NOTES FROM AUTHOR

This guide is intended for information purposes only. The author does not guarantee success nor is he responsible for any results brought about by the usage of the information contained herein for Dowsing is an Art and the skill of the Dowser and the will of God rule.

8 - LEGAL NOTICE

This skill is esoteric. If you have any mental, medical, physical or chemical diminishment presently, use of this technique is not recommended.

This method does not guarantee that anyone will dowse correctly and thereby know the answers correctly and get the maximum outcome that one could desire.

USE THIS INFORMATION AT YOUR OWN RISK.

The author shall not be held liable for any improper or incorrect use of the information described and contained herein and assumes no responsibility for any use of the information. In no event shall the author be liable for any direct, indirect, incidental, special, exemplary, or consequential damages.

9 - Thank You

For
Considering
These
Ideas

10 - Don't Worry Ever

Ever

It Does Not Help Prayer Still Does!

11 - Resource Books

Distant Healing Sessions (or Join Mail List) – Write To mikewann@voicenet.com

Books by Rev. Mike at **www.Amazon.com**

Veterans Healing Six Pack
1. Trauma Healing Options for VA Hospitals: Help for Veterans to Own Their Healing and their future.
2. Trauma Healing Action Steps for Veterans: Help to Start Healing
3. Trauma Healing Action Steps for Veterans: Empowerment
4. Trauma Healing Action Steps for Veterans: Forgiveness
5. Trauma Healing Action Steps for Veterans: Thought Freedom
6. Tea For Veterans: Welcome One Home

PTSD Power Pack:
1. The PTSD Project: Turn Pain To Power
2. PTSD & Soul Retrieval: Putting One Back Together
3. PTSD & The Purple PAD: Calling all Scientists and PTSD Patients

Angel Raphael Speaks Volume 1: Take Courage! God Has Healing in Store for You!
Angel Raphael Speaks Volume 2: Take Courage! God Has Healing in Store for You!
Angel Raphael Speaks Volume 3: Take Courage! God Has Healing in Store for You!
Angel Raphael Speaks Volume 4: Angels, Addicts, Alcoholics & Prisoners – Oh Yeah!
Angel Raphael Speaks Volume 5: Prisoners Caring for Alcoholics - Australia In Miniature Projects Intro
Angel Raphael Speaks Volume 6: Prisoners Caring for Addicts - Australia In Miniature For Addicts
Reiki Journaling from Japan
Reiki Is Alive: God's Great Gift
Four Parts to Healing
Distant Healing: We Are All Connected
Stress Release Energy Work: How To Cope
Does Reiki Love Heal Cancer?
Group Consciousness
Salute To Philadelphia VA Medical Center: Thank You
Reiki Transcript for Reiki 2 & 3 Channels: Dr. Usui Is That You?
God Bless Kindle & Amazon
Puppies Are Different From People
If Your Dog Dies
Toy Guns Are Obsolete

Great Spirit Made Children With Red Skin: AND
The Cage of Fear: Is Not Locked
God Made Children Red, Yellow, Brown, Black & White: Greet Each Child With Kindness
Emergency Medical Kindness In The Cradle Of Liberty: Big City - Cracked Bell
Angels Are Always Around Addicts and Addicts: Help Is Near Now! Invite It In!
Angels Are Always Around Addicts and Alcoholics: Volume 2 - Tools To Help Re-Light Your Life
Prison Jobs Now: Providing Care For Addicts And Addicts
Controlled Care Communities Concept
Prison Possibilities Dialogue Series: Concept
Prison Possibilities Dialogue Series: Volume 2, 3, 4, 5 Dialogues
Prison Possibilities Voluntary Exile
Prison Possibilities Corrections Coaches
Prison Possibilities For Mexicans: Is A Boat Better Than A Wall?
Prison Possibilities Family Time: A Reason to Thrive!
Prison Genius Pool: "So Much Genius In Jail."
Prison Possibilities Access Control: Prisoner Access by Request
Prisoner's Lawyers Can Save The American Economy: Make A Buck Doing It & Be Thanked!
Prisoner Family Talks, Days, Stays & Vacations: Connecting Helps Healing
Prisoner Writing Projects: Write To Heal, Start Over & Reconnect
Prison Cell Clearing & Blessing: Clear Entities, Chase Ghosts, and & Create Sacred Space
Prisoner Professors: Show You Are Aware Create Change With Care
Prison Reiki? Maybe Someday? A Gateway To Help Heal Prisons & America?
Judges and An Angel Rule On Possibilities: We Can Cut Sentences & Prison Costs
Ideas For Prison Wardens: Leadership Is Not Easy
Solitary Community: Could Community Support Cut Costs and Issues?

Little Books at Kindle.com by Rev. Mike:
English Medical History Questionnaire For Non-English Speakers
English Language Helper For Non-English Speakers
Wise Wonderful Women Are The Well Of The Family
Answers for Test & Research: Dowsing Power
Crisis? Reiki! Baby? Reiki!
Bible References For Healing
Angel Raphael Speaks – Prisons
Angel Raphael Speaks – Veterans
The Saint Off Interstate 95

12 - Angels Please Prayers

Addict's

Angels of Healing Selected
Help Me to Stay Directed
Come To Me From The Sky
I Am Ready to Succeed Not Try
If I Don't Invite You In
I Might Not Win
I Have Been Lost For Too Long
Help Me To Stay Strong

Alcoholic's

Angels of Healing On High
Help Me to Stay Dry
Come To Me From The Sky
I Am Ready to Succeed Not Try
If I Don't Invite You In
I Might Not Win
I Have Been Lost For Too Long
Help Me To Stay Strong

From

13 - Private Channeling

Angel Raphael Speaks a series of free messages that are channeled through Reverend Mike Wanner for the Highest good and Highest Healing of all concerned.

Many questions arise about Reverend Mike doing private channeling, and he does help with that so e-mail him.

Reverend Mike is available worldwide as a psychic channel, emotional release facilitator, spiritual energy practitioner & teacher, and public speaker. He looks forward to meeting you soon!

Email - mikewann@voicenet.com 215-342-1270 PRIVATE SPIRITUAL READINGS/channelings or Spiritual Healing Sessions: Telephone or in person. Rev. Mike is available for private, one-on-one intuitive sessions with you, his Guide Family, and your Guides. He helps by offering clarity on emotional situations about your life, your purpose, your spirituality, and the release of stuffed emotions and cellular memory.
Connect to the love of your Guides today!
Contact Rev. Mike for an appointment.

Sessions available:

Spiritual Readings
Angel Channeling
Distant Reiki Healing
Remote Clearing of Stuffed Emotions
Distant Clearing Cellular Memory
Distant Clearing Energy Blockages
Remote Clearing of the Chakras
Customized needs
Mastermind dowsing responses to yes/no direction finding questions.

Rev. Mike is a facilitator of healing. He brings you and the Divine together so that you can align with the Divine and have a great time and a great life. All healing is between you and God, as it should be. Go ahead and start without Rev. Mike. Visit his prayer site http://www.Create-A-Prayer.com. Take the first step NOW.

14 - Reverend Mike Wanner

Rev. Mike Wanner started his Metaphysical and Ministerial studies with Reiki in 1993 and had studied seven styles of Reiki in the U.S., Japan, Canada, Denmark and Australia. He is certified to teach. He became certified to teach Integrated Energy Therapy in 1999 and co-taught the first IET class of the new Millennium. Mike began dowsing in 2001.

Ordained as a Metaphysical Minister of the International Metaphysical Ministry and an Interfaith Minister of the Circle of Miracles Ministry, Rev. Mike practices and teaches spiritual energy therapies in the Philadelphia Area.

Rev. Mike holds ministerial degrees from the University of Metaphysics and the University of Sedona. He is a Pastoral Care Associate of Aria - Frankford Hospital. He taught at the National Academy of Massage Therapy and Health Sciences.

Rev. Mike was a faculty member of the Medical Mission Sister's Center for Human Integration's School of Integrated Body/Mind Therapies in Fox Chase, Philadelphia, PA for twelve years.

Rev. Mike is licensed by the teaching of Intuitional Metaphysics to practice Spiritual Healing and Scientific Prayer. Mike is also a Prayer therapist.

Rev. Mike was elected in 2007 to the status of "Fellow of the American Institute of Stress."

In 2008, Rev. Mike became a practitioner of Coincidental Recognition as he incorporated the CoRe System into his spiritual healing practice.

In 2009, Rev. Mike trademarked a new healing process called Quantum Quatro! Subtle Energy System Support®.

In 2011, Rev. Mike joined the outreach program known as the Health Advantage Group.

In 2012, Rev. Mike became a Certified Professional Coach by The Master Coaching Academy and Joined the Personal Empowerment Group.

Before his Metaphysical, Ministerial and Coaching studies, Rev. Mike worked for Sears Roebuck and Co. while in High School and after graduation, until he joined the U. S. Air Force in 1965. He returned to Sears from Vietnam in 1969 and stayed until 1978. His final Sears assignment was as an efficiency expert in Methods - Operational Research and Development.

He volunteered with Burholme Emergency Medical Services from 1969 and is still a Life Member and Board of Directors Member. He started a private ambulance company in 1975 and worked professionally in the field until 2001 when he devoted his full attention to real estate investing, healing, coaching, and writing.

www.ingramcontent.com/pod-product-compliance
Lightning Source LLC
Chambersburg PA
CBHW050037230526
45470CB00003B/1320